Let's Look at
Pigeons

Janet Piehl

Lerner Publications Company
Minneapolis

For everyone who likes pigeons

There are many kinds of pigeons. This book focuses on rock pigeons.

Lerner Publications Company
A division of Lerner Publishing Group, Inc.
241 First Avenue North
Minneapolis, MN 55401 U.S.A.

Website address: www.lernerbooks.com

Library of Congress Cataloging-in-Publication Data

Piehl, Janet.
    Let's look at pigeons / by Janet Piehl.
        p.   cm. — (Lightning bolt books™ – Animal close-ups)
    Includes index.
    ISBN 978-0-8225-7897-0 (lib. bdg. : alk. paper)
    1. Pigeons—Juvenile literature. I. Title.
    QL696.C63P54 2010
    598.6'5—dc22   2007029224

Manufactured in the United States of America
1 2 3 4 5 6 — BP — 15 14 13 12 11 10

Contents

Meet the Pigeon

What kind of birds do you see in the city?

These birds live near buses, cars, tall buildings, parks, and busy people.

You see pigeons in the city!

Pigeons gather in groups called flocks. You may see flocks of pigeons in city parks, on sidewalks, and under bridges.

Pigeons perch on a city bridge.

Pigeons also live outside cities. Some live on farms. Others live on cliffs in the mountains or near the ocean.

This pigeon lives on a cliff above the ocean.

Pigeon Bodies

Many pigeons have gray feathers covering their bodies. They have colorful feathers on their necks.

Pigeons have round bodies.
Their eyes are
red or orange.
Their small heads bob
when they walk.

Pigeons have
excellent eyesight.

Pigeons are strong flyers.

Strong wings help pigeons fly fast. Pigeons can fly 40 to 50 miles (64 to 80 kilometers) per hour. That is almost as fast as a car on the highway.

Pigeons can fly long distances. Some can fly as far as 600 miles (965 km) in a day. That is like flying from the top of the state of Florida to its tip.

Pigeons use their strong wings to fly away from predators. Predators are animals that hunt and eat other animals. Falcons and hawks are predators of pigeons.

A peregrine falcon chases a pigeon.

Some people dislike pigeons. They do not like flocks of birds living near them. They chase pigeons away.

Other people like pigeons.
They feed them seeds,
peanuts, and bread crumbs.

A boy feeds
pigeons in a
city park.

City pigeons will eat almost anything!

They eat food thrown away by people. Pigeons also eat grains and fruits.

Pigeons Build Nests

Coo! Coo! This pigeon is looking for a mate. He makes a cooing sound to attract a female.

These two pigeons are ready to start a family. They must find a place to build a nest.

Have you ever seen a pigeon nest?

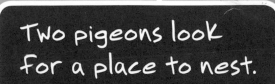

Two pigeons look for a place to nest.

Most people have never seen a pigeon nest. Pigeons build their nests where predators cannot find them.

City pigeons build nests on tall buildings and under bridges. Other pigeons build nests high on cliffs.

This pigeon nested high above a city street.

The pigeon's nest is small. It is made of loose twigs and grasses. The female pigeon lays one or two white eggs in the nest.

Pigeons usually lay two eggs.

The male and the female both incubate the eggs. This means they keep them warm. The eggs hatch after about eighteen days.

Pigeons sit on their eggs to incubate them.

How Pigeons Grow

Baby pigeons are called squabs. They have fuzzy yellow feathers. They cannot see or fly.

The pigeon parents feed the squabs pigeon milk.

These squabs
are hungry.

Pigeon milk comes from a pigeon's crop. The crop is a sack inside the bird's throat.

All pigeons' throats contain a crop to feed their young.

The parent opens its mouth. The squab sticks its head inside to drink the milk. The milk helps the squab grow quickly.

A pigeon feeds its squab.

Soon, the young pigeons are ready to leave the nest. They are ready to find food on their own.

These pigeons look for food in the city.

The pigeons fly past buses, cars, tall buildings, parks, and busy people. Do you see pigeons where you live?

Fun Facts

- Pigeons live all over the world. They can be found everywhere except the Arctic, Antarctica, and certain islands.

- About three hundred different kinds of pigeons exist.

- Pigeons suck water through their beaks when they drink, just as you might use a straw to drink!

- One type of pigeon is known for its ability to find its way home from far away. This type of pigeon is called the homing pigeon. People sometimes use homing pigeons to deliver messages.

Pigeon Diagram

eye

head

beak

tail

feathers

wing

claw

foot

Glossary

crop: a special sack inside a pigeon's throat. Pigeon milk is produced there.

flock: a group of pigeons

incubate: to keep warm. Pigeons must incubate their eggs so that they will hatch.

pigeon milk: a liquid that pigeons feed to their babies. It comes from a pigeon's crop. It helps young pigeons grow strong.

predator: an animal that hunts and eats other animals

squab: a baby pigeon

Further Reading

Boring, Mel. *Birds, Nests and Eggs.* Minocqua, WI: NorthWord Press, 1996.

Project PigeonWatch
http://www.birds.cornell.edu/pigeonwatch

Rock Pigeon
http://www.enature.com/fieldguides/detail
.asp?shapeID=968&curGroupID=1&lgfromWhere=&
curPageNum=4

Silverman, Buffy. *Do You Know about Birds?* Minneapolis: Lerner Publications Company, 2010.

Sill, Cathryn. *About Birds: A Guide for Children.* Atlanta: Peachtree, 1997.

Index

Photo Acknowledgments

The images in this book are used with the permission of: © Jeffrey Banke/Dreamstime.com, p. 1; © Martin Spurny/Dreamstime.com, p. 2; © Jan Richter/Dreamstime.com, p. 4; AP Photo/ Frank Franklin II, p. 5; © Kim Karpeles/Alamy, p. 6; © Andrew Darrington/Alamy, p. 7; © Spencer Platt/Getty Images, p. 8; © Destinyvispro/Dreamstime.com, p. 9; © blickwinkel/ Alamy, p. 10; © John Foxx/Stockbyte/Getty Images, p. 11; © Jim Zipp/Photo Researchers, Inc., p. 12; © Daniel Attia/zefa/CORBIS, p. 13; © Ryan McGinnis/Alamy, p. 14; © Philippe Clement/ naturepl.com, p. 15; © WILDLIFE/Peter Arnold, Inc., p. 16; © Donald Enright/Alamy, p. 17; © Mike Lane/Alamy, p. 18; © Laurent Geslin/naturepl.com, p. 19; © Jose Luis GOMEZ de FRANCISCO/naturepl.com, p. 20; © Neil Bowman/FLPA, p. 21; © Heidi & Hans-Jürgen Koch, pp. 22, 23, 25; © Inaki Relanzon/naturepl.com, p. 24; © Jareso/Dreamstime.com, p. 24; © Mitchell Funk/Photographer's Choice/Getty Images, p. 26; © Florian Kopp/imagebroker.net/ Photolibrary, p. 27; © Dimitry Maslov/Dreamstime.com, pp. 28, 31; © Laura Westlund/ Independent Picture Service, p. 29; © Soleg1974/Dreamstime.com, p. 30.

Front cover: © Peter Arnold/Alamy.